BEGIN YOUR DAY WITH A SMILE AND 7 MANTRAS TO INCREASE YOUR HAPPINESS

DR. MANORAJ KOTI

Copyright © Dr. Manoraj Koti
All Rights Reserved.

* This book is dedicated to everyone and

Special thanks to my Family who supported me for my
Writings ! *

Contents

Foreword

This book has been written for information purposes only. Every effort has been made to make this Book as complete and accurate. Therefore, this Book should be used as a guide - not as the ultimate source. The purpose of this Book is to educate. The author and the publisher do not warrant that the information contained in this book is fully complete and shall not be responsible for any errors or omissions. The author and publisher shall have neither liability nor responsibility to any person or entity with respect to any loss or damage caused or alleged to be caused directly or indirectly by this Book.

Preface

Dr. Manoraj Koti

Dr. Manoraj koti, has done his masters in psychology and persuing as counselling psychologist. He also loves to explore and intrepret the people mindset and nature and tries to work how he can help the people, who is suffering from mental health. he also love to intrepret in writings ..

Inside this book, you will discover the topics about do you need money to be happy, dont sweat the small stuff, how happy are you - questions to ask yourself, the link between food and happiness, seven mantras to increase your happiness, why living in the moment makes you happier, hormones and happiness, etc..

Introductory

Sometimes we make dramatic plans that are expected to bring happiness into our lives, whether it be a vacation, graduation or wedding.

But the simple pleasures in life are what we can count on to give us continuous joy. When we appreciate and enjoy the simple things, the gratitude we feel will extend to other areas as well. Here are some of the simple pleasures that are worth making an effort to experience often.

Freshly Cut Grass

Freshly cut grass is enjoyable in every way. The smell and feel of it under your bare feet are fresh, and invigorate the senses. Try to experience this at least a few times each year, as the weather allows it.

Giving and Receiving Smiles

What a better way to experience a simple pleasure for free? Give smiles not only to your friends, but also to random strangers you pass on the street. You will be amazed at how good it feels to see first the surprise of others, and then their own smile in return.

The Endorphin Rush after Working Out

When you work out in a strenuous manner, you will get an endorphin rush as a reward. These natural, feel-good chemicals are sure to brighten your day. Work out in the morning in order to use this endorphin rush to help you be especially productive throughout the rest of your day.

Enjoying Your Favorite Food

Even if your favorite food is not especially healthy, allow yourself to have it every now and then. The feeling of your much-loved food will bring you a little boost of pleasure. Studies have shown that if you refrain from a particular food for a certain time, it will be even more enjoyable the next time you try it, so use this trick to make your favorite meal taste even better than usual.

Hot Cup of Coffee or Tea

Some of us survive on our daily coffee or tea. Even when it is a daily habit, it can bring much joy. As you sip on your beverage of choice, take some quiet time to enjoy every bit.

Making Snow Angels

This is not only for kids. Put on some warm clothes and simply fall into the snow. Feeling silly about this will not ruin the experience, just embrace the feeling of innocent fun that making snow angels can bring.

Laughing until It Hurts

Laughter is like medicine. Everyone should have an opportunity to laugh until it hurts at least once a day. Whether it is with a friend who could write comedy, or watching a good movie, take some time to laugh away your stress.

Getting a Massage

If you have never had a massage, give it a try. This hour of total relaxation will make your troubles feel as though they are melting away. Many individuals are even entitled to massages through employee benefits.

Walking in the Rain

Walking in the rain is one of life's amazing simple pleasures. Dress warm, and go outside with or without an umbrella. Let the rain splash over your face as you stroll along, and be sure to jump in at least one puddle for old time's sake.

Expensive fun is great, but can be hard to come by. Instead of waiting for your next vacation, indulge in one of these simple pleasures. By learning to appreciate the little things right next to you, you will find great fulfillment each and every day.

CHAPTER ONE

Do You Need Money to Be Happy?

As the saying goes, "Money can't buy you happiness." Or can it? Having a sufficient amount of money can certainly lower stress, but having an excess of it will not make you happier than anyone else.

So, can money buy you happiness or not? Here are a few thoughts to ponder on the subject.

Money Can Buy You a Limited Amount of Happiness

Studies have shown that yes, having enough money to meet your needs and those of your family does bring happiness. People living in poverty are generally less happy than those whose needs are met. Being able to pay for your bills and having enough to get by financially will help you succeed in feeling happy.

Excess Money Doesn't Equal Excess Happiness

Having more money than you need, however, will not bring you extra happiness. Money and happiness are not proportional. Someone with enough money to buy a large house and several cars will not necessarily have more happiness than another individual with exactly what they need.

Money Brings Stresses of Its Own

There is stress that goes along with having money. Whether you have a little or a lot, you likely know about this stress. There is the stress of knowing you need to spend what you have wisely, as well as the fact that people with ulterior motives are drawn to those who are financially wealthy.

Not About What Comes in But What Goes Out

It is not so much the amount of money that you make that ensures your happiness, but about what you are spending it on and where it is going on the way out. There are some principles for using money that can help you to feel more satisfied. Where you put your money and who receives it can make a difference as to whether you gained something by having had it.

Spend on Experiences, Not Things

Buying more things is not proven to make a person happy. Although investing in items that will last seems like a wise move, studies show that we tend to adjust to what we obtain. Having these things doesn't continue bringing unlimited happiness.

We are more likely to have long-term happiness when money is spent on experiences which will give us lasting memories. Whether this means going on vacation by yourself or with your family, or making time to do something fun every now and then... be sure to create experiences rather than purchasing something that will simply fade away over time.

Give It Away

Giving is one of the most satisfying things you can do with your money. Whether it is to charity or a friend in need, find a way to give back and share what you have. This is a way to spend that will bring long-term personal rewards.

The short answer is no; you do not need money to be happy. Money can be useful, however, to prevent stress that can diminish the happiness that you do have. No matter what amount of money you have, use these tips to help achieve the level of happiness you desire, and live a life filled with joy.

Don't Sweat the Small Stuff

We have all heard that we shouldn't sweat the small stuff. Letting oneself get stressed out over the little things in life is one of the biggest ways to bring unnecessary grief into life's path.

We can avoid a lot of negative feelings, and even health problems, simply by learning not to let the little things get to us.

Focus on the Big Picture

When something small happens that makes you want to rage, compare the moment's significance to everything else going on in your own life, and in the world around you. You may have spilled your cake batter on the floor an hour before your guests are due to arrive. Are your friends still going to love you and enjoy the evening even if you don't have a freshly baked cake for them? If so, maybe you should put your energy somewhere other than berating yourself for this small mistake.

Remember That We All Make Mistakes

When something small threatens to destroy your attitude and positive outlook, think about the fact that everyone makes mistakes. Whether it is yourself or someone else who caused the situation that feels like a train wreck, keep in mind that mistakes are a normal part of life that happen to everyone. Don't let one bad moment take you by surprise.

Forgive Others

It can be hard to forgive someone else when it feels like they have brought you extra work and stress. When someone rear ends your vehicle, you may be tempted to lash out at them verbally. However, stop and think about how it may feel to be in their situation. Don't act and feel as though you have never made a mistake, but choose empathy.

Forgive Yourself

Forgiving others can be a simple matter in comparison to forgiving ourselves. There are many moments that we treat ourselves worse than we would ever allow a friend to treat us.

When you are having a difficult time forgiving yourself, think of how you would handle a similar mistake made by a good friend. Stop and think before bullying yourself, and consider seeking professional help if you can't stop a cascade of negative thoughts every time you fall short of perfection.

Ask Yourself If It Will Matter in Ten Years

We all have problems, and generally at the time, any problem seems big. Perception is not always the truth, though, and it is up to us to put our situation into perspective so that we can properly deal with whatever comes our way.

When something negative happens in your life, ask yourself if it will matter in ten years. If it won't, let it go. If someone gives you the middle finger in traffic, you may be tempted to lose your cool, but it is simply not worth it. Save your emotions for things that are life changing and deserve your full attention.

When something goes wrong, you have two choices. You can slip into a rage, or let it go. Making the choice not to sweat the small stuff will bring your life-changing happiness, and you will be thankful for your own shift in perspective.

CHAPTER THREE

How Happy Are You? – Questions to Ask Yourself

A desire to be happy is something that almost everyone has in common. But it is not always easy to create happiness, nor to decide whether you are happy once you feel you should be in this particular state of mind.

Every life will have ups and downs, and so it is helpful if we have a gauge by which to judge whether we have achieved happiness or not.

Do I Wake Up Excited about the Day?

This is a tell-tale sign about your inner happiness. Do you wake up each morning ready to face the day, or do you feel anxious and fearful? It is difficult to be happy if you are starting off each morning in a negative way.

Do I Look Forward to My Main Occupation?

Whether you are working, attending school, or doing something else... you should feel a sense of anticipation when you think about being there. There are certain things we must do, like pay the rent, so your decision to work may not be an option. You do, however, have an option as to where you work. If you don't like it, change it.

Do I Enjoy the People I Spend Most of My Time With?

The people you spend the majority of your time with are the people who will have the greatest influence on you. If they are bitter, discouraging and lack motivation, chances are that you eventually will become the same type of person. If your friends are not uplifting, find new ones. Spend your extra time with those who will cause your life to be more joyful, and will help you create positive memories that will bring long-term happiness.

Do I Like Who I Am?

A key component to happiness is liking and loving yourself for who you are. If you don't, then you need to figure out why. Make necessary changes, and then choose to love yourself despite your flaws.

Do I Dread or Look Forward to My Future?

Happiness includes feeling confident and secure about your future. We live in uncertain times, but that doesn't mean that we have to live every day in fear. Grow your confidence in small ways, and consider counselling if you feel more than occasional stress when you think about the future ahead.

Do I Know My Life Purpose?

Everyone has a life purpose. There is something about you that makes you a unique gift to the world. If you have not discovered this about yourself yet, your self-esteem will suffer, as will your happiness. There are many questionnaires and books dedicated to discovering your life purpose. Consider investing your time to learn more and find what makes you feel most fulfilled in life.

Being happy is not a frivolous desire. It is important to know how you are wired and what it takes to be happy with yourself and your life. By asking yourself these questions and then taking a moment to think about your answers, you will be well on your way to a life of true happiness.

CHAPTER FOUR

The Link Between Food and Happiness

Did you know that food can greatly affect your mood, for better or for worse?

When it comes to happiness and every other area in your life, food has the capacity to harm or heal. By learning about what foods to choose and avoid, you will be able to help your body and mind, and embrace happiness.

Foods to Boost Happiness

So you want to use what Mother Nature has to offer in order to boost your mood? Start off with looking for foods that are high in healthy fats. Our brains rely on these fats, such as omega-3 fatty acids, and they do wonders for mood and improving happiness by allowing nerve cells to communicate more efficiently.

Walnuts, pumpkin seeds and fish oil are a great way to consume these. Omega-3 fatty acids have been proven to be as effective as common antidepressant drugs in regards to depression.

Berries are another wonderful way to boost your happiness. They contain anthocyanins, which are helpful to your brain as they support its function. Oranges, raw peppers and kiwi are high in Vitamin C which battles stress. Leafy greens boost your folic acid intake, and even dark chocolate is known to be a positive mood enhancer. Bananas and dates are easily found foods that are known to affect serotonin levels positively.

Your mood and mental function are also greatly affected by dehydration, so be sure to stay well-hydrated by consuming plenty of water.

Foods That Steal Your Joy

Sugar is the number one food to avoid if you wish to be happy. Sugar sets you up for a quick, false surge of energy when you feel the sugar high, which is then followed by a crash. Sugar can also harm your immune system and trigger depression.

Coffee has been known to lead to anxiety, which will also rob you of joy. Wheat prevents serotonin from being produced, therefore contributing to depression. Alcohol is linked with moodiness, and although some individuals feel temporarily euphoric after consuming it, the feeling generally fades into negativity.

Supplements to Consider

Vitamin C has been shown to reduce cortisol, which is the hormone that causes stress. Unless you are getting a substantial amount of this vitamin from your diet, a daily supplement is a good idea.

Because a folic acid deficiency has been linked to depression, you should consider taking a supplement. Omega-3 fatty acids and vitamin B12 are also helpful for a natural mood boost. Supplements that will help you control unhealthy cravings include vitamin B complex, Co-Enzyme Q10 and resveratrol.

Because food has such a big effect on your mood, you would be wise to utilize it to its full potential. Instead of just choosing your meal based on what you desire at the moment, turn your plate into a powerful weapon that will fight depression and anxiety, and build and maintain your happiness.

You deserve the chance to feel joy, and by modifying your eating habits you can change your life for the better. Choose your mood by choosing your food, and see the difference it makes.

CHAPTER FIVE

Seven Mantras to Increase Your Happiness

There are many ways you can increase your happiness, and several tricks that don't require much preparation or effort.

Our words have power, and by repeating mantras to yourself throughout your day, you will find that feeling happy begins to come naturally to you. Here are seven mantras that, when repeated often, can change your life.

I Am Amazing

These three words can help prevent you from falling into a slump of self hatred. Too many individuals do not have respect for themselves and forget that they are amazing, beautiful and one of a kind. Repeat this mantra often so the words will come to you when you need them the most.

I Am Grateful

Gratefulness is a sure way to gain happiness. When you are grateful, you are making an effort to remind yourself of the good things in your life. In turn, this positive attitude attracts even more good things.

I Love Myself at All Times

One of life's most important lessons is to love ourselves. If you feel as though you haven't quite gotten to a point of full self-love and respect, then repeat these words until you do. Say them when you are pleased with yourself, as well as when you are angry and disappointed in yourself.

I Am a Magnet to Good Things

Believing that good things and positive situations are headed your way, will actually help them do so. Thinking of yourself as a magnet to everything that is amazing will draw those things to you. Your self-confidence and positive spirit attract what they put out, and you will see your life becoming enriched as you repeat this mantra often.

I Attract Healthy People into My Life

Even in the best circumstances, the wrong people will keep us from going far. Create a circle of friends who are hopeful and positive just as you are. Avoid drama, and repeat this mantra to yourself when you are tempted to get sucked into someone's negative energy.

I Can Do Anything I Set My Mind To

Believing in yourself and having confidence in what you can achieve will take you far. When you know that you can do anything you set your mind to, you will find unlimited happiness in that knowledge. Speak these words when you are struggling to change your situation, and know that you have the power it takes to do so.

I Have a Purpose

No matter how much money a person makes or how much they accomplish, life will feel pointless and void without a sense of purpose. There are plenty of books written on the subject that can help you analyze your life and find out what your specific purpose is.

Think about the things you love and are drawn to, and what gives you your greatest feeling of satisfaction. You have something special to offer the world, and this mantra reminds you of that fact.

Our words hold much power, and mantras are a great way to set us on the path to happiness. When you use your words to bring positive things into your life, you will find happiness. Repeat these mantras and find out what a difference they will make for you.

Personality and Happiness

It appears that some people are just happier than others. It's not always just the people who have easy lives, either. Those who are happy seem to have certain factors that another individuals lack.

One definite factor is personality type. How does it play into the matter of personal happiness? Here are a list of personality traits and how they affect your feeling of well-being.

Perfectionism

Those personality types who lean towards perfectionism in relation to themselves and others, have a tendency to be less happy than those who are more accepting of various outcomes. Although a perfectionist will achieve happiness in a job well done, it will be limited due to their immediate focus on the next big project.

When you learn to enjoy the process rather than holding yourself to a strict set of rules, your happiness will grow.

Dreaming

Dreamers tend to be happy. Although dreamers can often lean towards procrastination, which brings stress, there is always something to dream about again after the stress has passed.

If we are not born this way naturally, we can learn a lot from dreamers as we seek happiness in life. Think about what you want out of life and spend a little time each day enjoying the thought of that very thing, and you will see the joy that can be found in this simple exercise.

Organization

People whose personalities lean towards being organized have a lot going for them, but it is possible to have too much of a good thing even in this area. The importance is in balance. Be too focused on organization and you will miss the small details that should be enjoyed along the way. By being too disorganized, on the other hand, you will experience the frustration of yourself and others when things do not go as planned.

Strike a happy medium, and choose to organize yourself just enough to make things work more efficiently.

Positivity

Positivity is one personality trait that absolutely affects one's personal happiness. Some people are born with a tendency to this trait, while others have to strive not to live in negativity.

No matter what side you lean towards naturally, make choices that will cause you to react in a positive manner and that will build your confidence in the process of life. You will find happiness comes to you naturally when you allow your energy to be transformed from negative to positive.

Living in the Moment

You may be an extrovert or an introvert, but whichever you are, you can choose to live in the moment. We only live our life through one time, and finding happiness includes being fully present for each and every step of the journey.

Some people find this easier to do, and others have to make an effort. Whatever your natural tendency, make a choice to do everything whole heartedly so that you will have no regrets and can experience deep happiness.

We can't change our personalities, but we can learn from each other. People with different personalities and personality traits have a natural inclination both towards and away from happiness. Take the personality you have been given and then direct your energy into living a happy life in the best way possible.

CHAPTER SEVEN

Why Living in the Moment Makes You Happier

We all know that living in the past can drag a person down, but why? And what about living in the future?

We need balance, but living in the moment is something we must focus on if we are to lead happy lives. Living in the moment has been shown to be the best way to become and stay happy. Here is why.

We Can't Change the Past

Almost every one of us has regrets about something in our past, but there is nothing we can do to change it. Instead of wasting our moments and energy in lament over situations that are long gone and no longer in our control to change, we can use the energy to make our present situation better. Learn what you can from the past, and then move on.

We Can't Predict What the Future Holds

Don't worry about the future, because you cannot predict what it will bring. You can only prepare to a certain extent, and being fearful about what tomorrow holds will only cause stress that will contribute to health and mental problems.

Live in the moment and choose to make the present your focus. Instead of fearing what repercussions your choices will bring to your future, make decisions based on what is good in your life right now at this moment. This will reduce tendencies towards depression and fear.

It Forces You to Be Present

When we think more about the past or the future than the present, we drift away from what is right in front of our eyes. Maybe your present involves a work project that demands your full attention and energy. Maybe your present involves small children with runny noses who need lunch put on the table.

When you embrace your present fully, you will get more out of the life you have. You will finally be able to stop sabotaging your present joy with fear about what may come next, or the guilt of decisions that are now in the past.

Be thankful for the faces in front of you now, and for the opportunities that are knocking on your door at this very moment. The moments you learn to cherish will enhance your future with the warm memories you will carry there, and you will have no regrets over misplaced focus.

Having a Balanced Outlook

Living in the present is important. Having a balanced focus is important too. When you think about the future, make the plans that are necessary for you to enjoy that time later, because someday the future will be your "in the moment." Don't neglect your planning for the future, but don't let it consume your life in an unhealthy way. Balance is key, and will help you not to feel stress due to too much focus on one area.

Living in the moment is one of the greatest things you can do for yourself. Happiness is achieved when we choose to live and enjoy where we are right now, instead of pining away for another time and place. By utilizing the time and the life you are given right here and now, you will know true happiness.

CHAPTER EIGHT

Hormones and Happiness

Hormones... they certainly don't get much respect at times. What do they have to do with happiness?

Actually, hormones play a big role in this feeling, and we are wise to learn about what factors they play in this area and what we can do to capitalize on them.

How Hormones Work

Hormones are special chemical messengers that control most of the body's processes. The endocrine glands create these special messengers and our body relies on them to function properly.

How we treat our bodies and the substances we surround ourselves with makes a difference in how these hormones are able to help us. By learning what they do and how we can assist them in doing their job, we will be closer to our goal of happiness.

What Hormones Are Related to Happiness?

There are several hormones that can boost one's happiness. The main ones include serotonin, oxytocin and dopamine.

Serotonin has become quite well known in recent times. It is a neurotransmitter, which takes messages from one part of the brain to another. Serotonin is crucial in preventing depression and other mental illness, and problems occur when you have either a shortage of this hormone or when it is unable to do its job.

Oxytocin is known as the "love hormone" and has a variety of jobs, which include helping people improve their social skills and minimizing fear.

Dopamine is another neurotransmitter, and it is activated when a positive and unexpected circumstance happens - which is why it is known for its role in helping the brain learn about rewards.

Natural Ways to Balance Your Hormones

Hormones need to maintain a fine balance in order to allow you to function at optimum levels. Too much or too little of any hormone will cause short and long-term problems health wise. Because our happiness is dependent on this, we are wise to do our best to find a healthy balance for all the hormones in our body, in order to create an environment that supports feeling good.

Some important ways to keep your hormones in good balance and working order are to get sufficient sleep each night, exercise regularly and eliminate toxins from your daily life. Minimize stress in your life as much as possible, and avoid birth control pills if possible.

Foods to Balance Your Hormones

Food plays an important role in the balance of hormones. There are many foods that you should make a point of eating on a daily basis, and many you should strive to avoid.

Foods and nutrients that help your body balance hormones and keep you happy include healthy fats such as those found in coconut oil, avocados, nuts and wild salmon. Vitamin D is an important supplement, as is magnesium. A sufficient amount of clean proteins should be eaten, as well as plenty of vegetables.

Your hormones play an essential role in your feelings of happiness. Keeping them balanced and working for you properly is important in order to ensure feelings of mental wellness. By following the guidelines above, you will be able to balance your hormones and live a life of happiness and satisfaction.